DEAR S.I.S
SCREAMING IN SILENCE?

Shamay Edmonds

Shamay Edmonds. © 2019

ISBN: 978-0-578-49289-6
Editors: P31 Publishing, LLC

Because of the dynamic nature of the internet, any web addresses or links contained in this book may have changed since publication and may no longer be valid. The views expressed in this work are solely those of the author and do not necessarily reflect the views of the publisher, and the publisher disclaims any responsibility for them.

Printed in the United States of America

To my mom, Grandma, aunt, cousins, to each of my bffs in any season, to the little girl that is trying to find herself, to my sis who is battling with insecurities yet no one would ever know it because of how you turned the scars into accessories I dedicate this to you all. To that grown woman who is so independent and doesn't need companionship only because of what companionship did to you... TO ALLLLLLL MY SISTERS IN CHRIST OR THOSE WHO ARE TRYING TO FIND HIM, OR THE ONES WHO THINK YOU DON'T NEED HIM...WHOEVER YOU ARE... YOU HAVE BEEN SCREAMING IN SILENCE FOR A WHILE NOW.... THIS IS FOR YOU.

So many times, the perceptions of people are misconstrued! How did that woman get so bitter? Why is she always lying? What makes her feel like she is better than anybody else? How is it someone so beautiful has absolutely no self worth? Well, prepare to get your mind blown! Everything is not always the way it seems, but a lot of it starts with betrayal, heartache, pain, lies, and deceit, but we have learned to live it in silence! Eventually, the chain will break my SIS!!!!

To you, the one who has learned to walk, cry, fall, and scream in silence.... This is for you!

Acknowledgement:

TO GOD BE ALL THE GLORY!!! GOD HAS DEFINITELY BLESSED ME BEYOND WHAT I COULD EVER IMAGINE! GREAT SHEPHERD AND FIRST Lady: Robert Lee Warren Jr, Mary Warren, great family and church family. You all are more than a pastor and First Lady, you both are a great set of Godparents. I would just like to say I Love you mother thank you for EVERYTHING, I understand now more than ever all the choices you had to make. Janet you are such a little big sister. You are such a role model for me and my children. You are by far one of the greatest people I know. Kae, girl I love you, you are truly one of my children even though we are sisters. You have set your standards in life high and for that I'm grateful. Quese and Tyrell you Know how much I love you all. Aunt Gloria you have taught me so much and I'm thankful for that, Uncle Buck you have always been there to guide me and show me unconditional love. I appreciate you all to the upmost!!!. My Whys of course: My children, Miyazaki (Mazak) Isaiah (Zae), Malachi(Mali) Josiah (JoJo) and Aaliyah (Lea Lea); You all are my babies, and you all make me better!!! Certainly last but not least, my biggest supporters, motivators, erasers of the naysayers... Rell (cousin but more like my older brother you have been there for me since I could remember. I can never repay you for that) Ebony (you are truly a best friend and a sister) we clicked so fast and have been on the same accord since then. You truly are a blessing from God. Ray (another best friend, it surprises me of how well you know me and how much we think alike. You are as honest as a person can be.I mean really honest and I love you for that. Mur (cousin girl as long as I've known you, you have always made me feel like a superhero and like I could do anything. Thank you so much. I could name so many more...BUT GOD TRULY GETS ALLLLLLLL OF THE GLORY

Dear S.I.S

How are you doing? I mean how are you really doing? When I wrote this book, I tried repeatedly to work on my introduction, but I just didn't seem to feel completely where I was going with it. Then, it hit me like a fastball meeting a baseball bat for the very first time. How could I bring my personality out to you... by just being myself? So, before you read this book, I just want to give you part of me, and part of me is putting you first. I want you to know that when God gave me the words to this book it was all for you, yes, you. See, I am very familiar with the most beautiful smiles and where they originate . After all, I have heard the phrase, "You have the most amazing smile!" all my life. So, I can attest to knowing exactly where a smile originates. A smile can be made of a thousand pieces of cuts, scrapes burns, backstabbing, brutality, abuse, and so much more. A beautiful smile can be birthed out of a dark and lonely space, but one thing I have learned about creating a lot of smiles is the best ones take practice with overcoming some type of secret pain. This pain can hurt so badly that you may feel like you can never share it with anyone or ever overcome it. It becomes embedded in your heart to the point that sometimes even you forget that it is there because you have perfected hiding it so well. However, in hiding this pain, it requires work, labor, and rehearsal. Rehearsal for what? Rehearsal to cover it up. Some cover it up with jokes, sarcasm, attitudes, and just make-up, but then you learn that the best cover up, the best way to keep people from trying to figure out your story, is to CREATE THE MOST DAZZLING SMILE. So, how can fake a smile that looks as real as it does? It is simple. You just go back to that innocent child before any hurt or danger or pain came your way, and you live off her. You use that same vision and imagination that said, "When I grow up, I'm going to be a princess with a big house, a strong husband, and the most beautiful kids. I'm going to be (whatever career your vision you selected), and I'm going to live happily ever after." You go to that place, and you pretend as though it all came true or was even better than what you imagined, and you run with that. The bad thing about that whole process is after you break out that smile, and everybody has gone and stopped looking at you, you have to go back to your place of honesty. You face the fact that the pain indeed is still there, and because no one is watching, you can actually take the smile off your face.

I've been there. Sometimes, if I'm not careful, I may still visit that place. That place is not like any other because if you are not really careful, you get stuck in that big web of that agony all over again. Have you ever heard of the saying, "It takes one to know one?" Well, that phrase is so true. That's why I can write these words with so much confidence because if you have never experienced this journey, believe me you have mothers, sisters, daughters, cousins, co workers and/or friends who are battling with this emotional web of hiding what they are really dealing with. So, understand that every single woman in this world may not relate to this story, but I guarantee they have worked hard to keep people from knowing something about an event or someone who has affected them in one way or another. This leads me to continue to reach out to you, yes, you. If you are reading this, something about the title, something about the cover, or something about what you may have heard about the book or about me has drawn you to give this book a chance. All I will say to that is...You are my S.I.S..., and in this book, you will truly find out what it means to be that S.I.S., that woman, that girl, who has done it or is doing it right now. Doing what? SCREAMING IN SILENCE

So, again I say Dear S.I.S., this is for you! I know you stand, you smile, you stumble, and sometimes you break, but if you are reading this, my S.I.S., you are still here! Because you are still here, know that I wrote this for you. As a woman, it is so hard to smile in the midst of it all, but you still do it. You may want to cry out for help or cry out, "Save me, fight for me, rescue me. Somebody, do something!" or even ask the Lord Jesus "Why me?" Well, I'm here for you. I have a message for you. If you think you are worse off than anybody, understand this somebody is going through the same thing or going through a worse battle than you. You don't believe me? I challenge you to read this book. It's filled with other women who smiled with all their brokenness. Some made it, and unfortunately, some didn't. This is not a fairy tale, but it is one of true events. SO OPEN YOUR HEARTS AND RECEIVE THE BATTLES OF THESE WOMEN WHO ALL WERE "SCREAMING IN SILENCE."

REFLECTIONS

_____

_____

_____

_____

_____

_____

_____

_____

_____

_____

_____

_____

_____

REFLECTIONS

_____

_____

_____

_____

_____

_____

_____

_____

_____

_____

_____

_____

1ST LET ME GIVE YOU A LITTLE OF THE BACKGROUND I WAS TALKING ABOUT….

When I reflect over my life, I am amazed how so many things that I overcame with God happened without knowing at the time it was God. I was going through different things during each era of my life. I thought I was cursed, cast out, and counted out; however, when I overcame it, I never knew how to cherish it. Well, that was until I met Jesus. Have you ever heard the phrase, "The prettiest smiles have been through the worst pain?" Well, I related to that more than I believe anyone could know.

I started acting when I was about 5 years old. I stayed with my grandmother who just happened to always have card parties on the weekend and sometimes on the weekday. Well, with her being popular for these parties, she always had different men and women coming there to gamble or drink gin shots. I now know better than I knew then that I had no business around these grown people when they came there. Sadly, I learned that the hard way. There are two people in this chapter of my life who stood out more than other people who impacted my life. Both of them were of the same class. They were older, black, drunk, miserable old men. Well, the first incident happened in the back room of my grandmother's house. This man used to come to my grandma's all the time. He would come and sit with her and also attend some of the card parties. He used to buy 2-4 shots of gin and sit with my grandmother and drink them as he talked about the type of day he had. His laugh matched his voice, and his voice was as deep as a baritone. At least, that's how I remembered it. Sometimes, he would bring me candy, and sometimes he would give me fifty cents to buy a soda. I always told him thank you and gave him a hug. He was such a nice man who always came around. Well, at least, that's what I thought. He came there on a night when my grandma didn't have a big turn out for a card night. In fact, it was only my grandmother and the old man. They played about 2 hands of Tunk, and then they were done. As the man was about to leave, my grandma went in her back room and started rocking in her rocking chair. She was eating a pork chop sandwich, I believe, and I followed the man to the front door to walk him out. Well, he decided he was not quite ready to go, so he sat in my uncle's chair in the front room. My uncle was at work. He sat down and just started talking to me. I remember him taking his baseball hat off and scratching his head. He had a bald head. He started asking me where was my little boyfriend who usually came around. I told him he wasn't my boyfriend. He was just my friend, and he was home with his mom. He then went on to tell me I was too pretty to have a boyfriend anyway. I asked him what did he mean. He went on to say this to me. He said, "Shamay, being pretty at a young age is a blessing and a curse. Too much attention is not good attention, and not enough attention is not necessary bad attention. You are a beautiful girl, and boys your age and older will only try to hurt you. Do you want to be hurt?" I remember replying with such innocence, "No, I never want to be hurt." He then went on to say, "As long as I'm here, you will never be hurt. Does that sound good to you? You want me to be your boyfriend?" I remember feeling confused and kind of scared, but I replied, "Yea, I'll let you be my boyfriend." When I said those few words, he smiled, and he told me to come here so he could tell me a secret. When I came closer, this is what he said, "Shamay, you are my girlfriend now, but it has to be our secret, so you can't tell your grandma or anybody else." He kissed me on my lips. When he kissed me on my lips his hands touched my face. I remember at that time, I didn't feel scared, but I felt like it was wrong. I asked him, and oh how I wished for so many years I didn't ask him this, but I did I ask him, "Why are your hands so big?" When I asked him that, he replied, "That's not the only thing that's big. Since you are my girlfriend now, I can show you something and not worry about you telling anybody about it. I want you to touch it first, and then I'll show it to you," I replied, "Ok," so then he took my hand and put it in his white, rusted pants. I remember asking him, "What is this and why is it so hard?" He told me with such calmness in his voice, "It's my other little friend, and since you are my girlfriend, you have to touch it, and rub it, and even kiss it, but remember, this is our secret." So after he said that, he grabbed my face and told me he was going to show me how to kiss his "little friend," and he took his tongue and put it in my mouth. He swirled it around, and he told me to do the same thing back. I did it, but at this point, I really felt so scared, but in my mind I was his girlfriend, and this is what I was supposed to do. After this, he said very proudly, "Very good job. Now, I want you to do the same thing to my little friend that's in my pants, but hold on, let me make sure no one can see us." He stood up, looked in the back room, and replied, "Ok, go ahead and kiss my little friend," and like a clueless little girl, I did it, but within 30 seconds, I heard my grandma calling me. When she called me, he jumped up, and he left, but before he left he said, "Don't forget, this is our secret because if anybody finds out about it, something really bad is going to happen to your grandma," so I listened to him. Even after my grandma called me and asked me where was I and what was I doing, and for some reason she even asked me was he still here and did he try to touch me, all I could do is remember what he said. I started my acting right then and there. Even after talking to her and thinking about the things she was asking me, I knew he had made me do something wrong, but I put the biggest smile on my face and I replied to her, "No, grandma. He didn't touch me" My grandma never knew what happened because all I could remember him saying was if I told anybody, something bad would happen to her. That was my first experience of "SCREAMING IN SILENCE"

PRELUDE: NOW, AT THIS POINT I KNOW A LOT OF MY FAMILY AND FRIENDS MAY BE SURPRISED TO HEAR THIS. IF THEY ARE READING THIS, LET ME JUST TAKE THIS MOMENT TO SAY THIS IS ABSOLUTELY NOT ABOUT YOU, BUT IT IS ABOUT WHAT GOD HAS PLACED ME TO DO. IF YOU ARE HEARING THIS FOR THE VERY FIRST TIME, IT'S OK. THAT DOESN'T TAKE AWAY ANY LOVE OR BOND WE HAVE, BUT THIS IS ABOUT HELPING MY READERS HEAL.

So, what was the second story? The second story isn't as bad and graphic as the first one, but it still required me to keep my mouth closed and keep this secret embedded in my heart. It still took away from who I was as a child, and it still traumatized me. Ready? Again, this was an event that took place at my grandma's house. This wasn't during the night. It was a Saturday morning. I was in the second grade, and I remember it so well because this was not only scary for me, but it was scary for him too. On Saturday mornings, my grandma used to wake up and fry some cornbread cakes, fatback, and eggs. After we ate breakfast, this man came to the door on crutches. He had been there before but not as much as my grandma's other acquaintances. He was a really sad drunk. He dressed sloppily, walked side-to-side, and always smelled like beer and grass. When he came in on this particular Saturday, he asked my grandma if he could buy a shot. She started fussing at him telling him she doesn't start selling this early and that he had to come back later. He practically begged her, and she eventually sold him two shots. After she poured it, he pulled out a stack of money, and I remember me saying, "You sure do have a lot of money." That was the end of the conversation. Well, my grandma said she had to go to the bathroom, and she moved around a little slowly, so when she went to the bathroom, everybody knew it was going to be a few minutes. When she went into the bathroom, he called me over to the table where he was sitting, and I sat down and said, "Yes." He replied, "So you think I got a lot of money, huh? Here is 7 dollars for you. Buy you something from the store." I said, "Thank you" with a smile on my face, and that's when it happened. He yanked my head and kissed me in my mouth. I tried to push him, but he was too strong. Violently, he said to me, "Don't push me away and don't think about telling anybody, or I will kill everybody in this house." I was crying and begging him to stop kissing me, and then I heard my grandma walking towards me. She asked me what was wrong because I was crying. I said in a crying and loud voice, "Nothing grandma." I remember her looking at me and then looking at him. Then, he came out his mouth and said, "You have you a fast lil granddaughter. I told her not to be talking to men the way she do, or somebody is going to take what they want from her." My Grandma then took the frying pan off the stove and she started beating him in the face with it, and told him he better not ever come back to her house, and she also told him that if she found out he did anything to me, she would kill him. He rushed out with his two crutches and yelled at me and said, "Remember what I said. I ain't playing with you!" From that moment on, my grandma never let me out of her reach or sight. She asked me over and over again, year after year, what happened that day, and each time I replied, "Nothing. I was just scared of him." During those moments when she would ask me what happened, I would want to tell her over and over again, but I had to keep it buried in my heart. I couldn't tell her or anybody else. I was in the second grade just "SCREAMING IN SILENCE."

TO MY S.I.S ALL OF YOU AND ALL MY READERS, UNDERSTAND THIS, I'M NOT WRITING THIS JUST TO SELL A BOOK. I'M WRITING THIS WITH MUCH UNDERSTANDING THAT EVERY SINGLE THING THAT GOES ON IN YOUR LIFE IS FOR A REASON. DON'T WASTE YOUR STORY IN SECRET OR EXCUSE IT BY THINKING IT WAS AN ACCIDENT. ALLOW THE THINGS THAT YOU HAVE BEEN THROUGH TO MAKE YOU STRONG, MAKE YOU BETTER, MAKE YOU ALIVE AND NOT DEAD, AND MAKE YOU USE YOUR STORY TO HELP OTHERS. SCREAMING IN SILENCE IS HERE TO SHOW YOU THAT YOU DIDN'T GO THROUGH THIS BY YOURSELF, AND YOU

DON'T HAVE TO CHOOSE THIS ROAD OF FAKING YOUR HAPPINESS. IN ACTUALITY, YOU CAN BE FREE AND HELP OTHERS. I AM MY BROTHER'S KEEPER AND MY SISTER'S KEEPER AS WELL. I JUST PRAY THAT THIS BOOK HELPS YOU OVERCOME YOUR SCREAMING. SO WITHOUT FURTHER ADO, I'D LIKE TO BEGIN BY TELLING YOU ABOUT SOME WOMEN I KNOW. THEY ALL EXPERIENCED

SCREAMING IN SILENCE

PERSONAL PRAYER

_____

_____

_____

_____

_____

_____

_____

_____

_____

_____

_____

_____

PERSONAL PRAYER

_____

_____

_____

_____

_____

_____

_____

_____

_____

_____

_____

_____

SCREAMING IN SILENCE......
THE YOUNG GIRL

A lot of adults said she was too grown. She was exposed to things that her eyes should not have seen, her ears should not have heard, and even her hands should not have felt. This young girl had always had challenges but never expressed them because the impression that others had of her was much better than what was really going on inside her. Although she was surrounded by family here and family there, this young girl felt so alone at all times. Have you ever felt that way? Have you felt like although you see so many faces that you know and voices that you are used to, but you hold so many secrets inside that you know no matter how much someone wants to know you or even think they know you they will never know who you really are because the secrets that you hold change your whole identity? Well, that's exactly how she felt. One night, this young girl was at a family member's house with other young girls. All the girl could do was admire how pretty the other girls were, how well put together they were, how well they could dress, and how confident they were about themselves. She remembered something her teacher said that week, "Think of what you want to be when you grow up and allow nothing to get in your way of becoming that." Well, at the time, she told her teacher that she couldn't think of anything, but that night being surrounded by all the young, confident, and pretty girls, she thought to herself, "Oh yea, when I get older, I'm going to be one of those girls. I'm going to look good, smell good, dress well, and be confident in myself." For that slight moment, she believed it. That was until reality set in. Then, she teared up briefly saying, "Yea right." That very night, the girls stayed up dancing and joking. The young girl had to blend in with the crowd no matter how uncomfortable she was. She danced liked them, talked like them, and even made up lies to relate to them. That night, when the girls laid down to sleep, she remembered how she was just so different and so ugly. She felt she was so out of place and wasn't formed like them. She laid down and tried to think of good thoughts, and then that's when it happened. The oldest out the bunch of girls (mind you they all were family) started to rub on her back saying, "I'm cold!" Girl (lets just begin to call her that for now) didn't think anything of it, and then she begin to feel the oldest girl rub on her even more. Surprisingly, girl didn't know exactly what to think. Well, that was until her hand was forced to go into the girl's shirt. After that, the oldest girl started telling her things to do, and well, Girl did it and didn't say anything about it. She just added the experience to other things she had to hold in like the time she was asleep at a best friend's house and she woke up in pain to the oldest brother fingering her forcefully and her just hearing his deep voice saying, "Shhhh!!! Don't say anything!" The thoughts that went through her mind that night were "Out of all the women you can get with because you aren't ugly, WHY AND WHAT WOULD YOU WANT WITH THIS 11-YEAR-OLD." It wasn't like "Girl" was surprised at the things that happened to her. She just became numb to them all not knowing how bad they were affecting her. However, what she learned out of all she experienced was how to put on the prettiest smile thru all the hell she went through. This was the second time in life she practiced the "SCREAMING IN SILENCE."

ENCOURAGEMENT

_____

_____

_____

_____

_____

_____

_____

_____

_____

_____

_____

_____

ENCOURAGEMENT

SCREAMING IN SILENCE....THE GIRL FRIEND

Have you ever watched a romantic movie on television and thought to yourself, "Wow!!! I wish I could find someone like that, or I wish I was that girl?" Then, when reality comes to play, you say "Well, that isn't even real.." Have you ever compared the way you were treated in a relationship to the relationships you see on television, and then someone crushed your feelings by letting you know that what you see on television is not real? Well, I knew this girl who we can call "Girl." She wasn't brought up like most girls. She never had a role model who taught her how a girl was suppose to be treated, so she began to watch a lot of television and determined from the movies what should make her happy and what shouldn't. She knew it would be hard to find it because who she was raised around were women who didn't know their identity, women who sold themselves, and violent women who weren't scared to cut a man if he said something wrong out of his mouth. She didn't discredit these women. She just came to her own conclusion that she did not want to become like them.

I remember "Girl" telling me a story about one time her uncle got so drunk that he fell asleep on the couch, and this lady who came to the house acted as if she wanted to lay on him, but what she really did was take his wallet and stole all his money. Well the next day, her uncle confronted the woman about it, and they were fussing and it got really bad. Immediately, the woman left out, and her uncle stormed out behind her. About an hour later, her uncle came back to the house stabbed severely. He had to be rushed to the emergency room and get treated. All "Girl" could do was cry and imagine how her life would be if she would ever become like this woman. The next morning, her uncle came home and told her, "Baby, no matter how drunk I get, I know how much of an angel you are. Don't you be like these crazy women who give it up to anybody for anything and do anything to get what they want. Remember, you are my angel." That conversation stuck with "Girl" even though she knew her uncle didn't have it all and was a drunk. She chose to take his sober moments and listen to what he had to say. That conversation followed her throughout life, and she didn't even realize it until her first relationship.

"Girl" had been in school for years, and when she got in 5th grade, she began to have a crush on a young boy who seemed to like her too. She would come home from school everyday and go to her neighbor's house to talk to the boy on the phone. They had good conversations, but every day when they got to school, the boy acted as though he didn't know her. She didn't really know what that was about until she found out that the boy had a girlfriend who was having sex with him. She soon came to the conclusion that he was ashamed of her and just wanted to have sex with her too. Girl got a little older and took the feeling of shamefulness with her to middle school. This was the era in her life during which she became the girlfriend but really wasn't the girl friend. "Girl" had moved and begun to hang with a boy who made her feel not so shameful. Although people didn't know they talked on the phone or came to each other's house just to joke around, this was the first boy who made her feel worthy of affection. He would come over, and they would sit on her steps. He would kiss her over and over again and make her get butterflies. "Girl" had never experienced anything like that before. This was the first time in life she felt like she was kissed like the girls she saw on the television.

One day, they were at the bus stop, and the other boys decided they wanted to joke on her. "Girl" couldn't believe she was being this tortured by words, and all the other boy would do is look at her. Finally, the boy said, "Hey fellas, y'all leave her alone." The boys started talking very low amongst each other. All of a sudden one of the young guys said, "Hey, we are sorry. Can we start over?" "Girl" agreed because she was a very forgiving person, and she just wanted to be loved and liked. Moments later, the boys asked if they come over and get something to drink. She let them come in and told them they had to hurry before her mom got there. The boys came in, and that's when it happened. The boys locked the door, and they began to push on her. Two of them laid her on the floor. They lifted her shirt up and started farting on her stomach with their mouths. She asked them over and over again to stop. One of them started licking on her neck while the other ones were holding her arms down. They snatched her bra off and started pinching on her breasts. The four boys including the boy she thought made her feel special. Suddenly, the oldest boy started to take her pants off, and "Girl" yelled at them asking them to please stop. They were laughing except the one who actually really did like her and came to see her almost everyday. As they were about to pull her underwear off, the one boy that she was close with said, "Fellas! Alright, let's stop! She has had enough! Let's leave her alone."

All the boys stopped, and the oldest one, the same one who took her pants off, said, "We will make a deal with you. If you don't tell anybody about this, we won't joke on you ever again, and when we see you in school, we will speak to you like we are friends." Shamefully, "Girl" agreed to it and never told anybody what happened that day. However, that day took part of her identity, and it followed her in almost every relationship until she was out of high school. She felt so inadequate with men that when she was presented with the option of a relationship, she went with it. No matter how they treated her, talked to her, or cheated on her, she stayed. She wanted someone to give her that feeling of love and security even when she knew it wasn't real. This was another moment in life where she had to swallow all the hurt and pain and practice acting, so she put on the prettiest smile and practiced "SCREAMING IN SILENCE."

REFLECTIONS

SHAMAY EDMONDS

REFLECTIONS

_____
_____
_____
_____
_____
_____
_____
_____
_____
_____
_____
_____

SCREAMING IN SILENCE....
THE SINCERE LYING FRIEND

Now, looking at this section, I know someone is asking, "What kind of friend can be a sincere liar as a friend?" I CHALLENGE YOU TO LOOK AT THIS SCENARIO! I am not making excuses for this young girl, but my heart goes out to this particular situation. There was a girl who only desired to feel wanted and loved. Have you ever been rejected as a child from a parent, grandparent, sibling, peer, or someone whom you just wanted to love you? Well, this girl was looking for someone to feel a void that it seemed could never be filled. This girl went about trying to fill the void in all the wrong ways. Have you ever met that person who seemed like he or she wanted to bend over backwards or forwards for you and always had the best advice, but later on you realized that it was too good to be true? Well, "Girl"was that person. Although she had a gigantic heart, she still had a lot of unresolved issues.

She had so many disappointments in life, and happiness, sincere and true happiness, seemed only like a fairy tale or a fictional story. She concluded that happiness was made up, so she decided in most areas in her life she would make up these fairytales and these fictional stories of her life. From the age of 6, her lies started as little baby lies. She went into her aunt's makeup to make herself look and feel pretty. She walked down the street in the middle of the night in a dangerous neighborhood to get attention. One time when she was 6 years old, she was in the house late at night, and her little play boyfriend was there. They started kissing, not just a pitty pat kiss but like the kisses you saw on cable television. She felt so loved and wanted at that time; however, she was way too young to be kissing on a boy. The young boy's older sister called her in another room to ask her why were they kissing, and immediately she denied it. She thought she was going to get in trouble, and then all of a sudden, the much older sister responded, "That's too bad because you knew what you were doing. I wanted to try it with you." Not knowing how to respond, she just smiled and nodded her head. Then, the older sister of the boy told her to come a little closer, and the older girl started rubbing on her hair and said softly, "Show me what you were doing with my brother, and I won't tell on y'all." "Girl" did what she was told, and everytime they came over to her house, the same thing happened repeatedly.

From that day, she decided people were going to do what they wanted to do regardless of what she said, so she made a conscious decision that no one would ever be able to handle her truth, so she would just say whatever they wanted to hear in the moment. "Girl" continued down this road until she lost really good friends and learned that all people weren't the same. She was scared so badly that she got to a point in her life in which she couldn't even distinguish when she lied and when she told the truth. "Girl" no longer had an identity. She was just like a ship without a sail. She was so tortured on the inside that she didn't really know who she was. All she could do was practice "SCREAMING IN SILENCE."

PERSONAL PRAYER

PERSONAL PRAYER

_____

_____

_____

_____

_____

_____

_____

_____

_____

_____

_____

_____

SCREAMING IN SILENCE
"THE MURDERER"

Being angry and filled with rage to the point where you don't even know that's how you are characterized is a scary thing. Have you ever talked to someone whom you knew and tried to tell him or her something that offends you that he or she does, and he or she has no recognition of it? Have you ever tried to express to that person how he or she may come off to other people, and he or she gets offended? Have they ever gotten so angry that he or she says cruel and hateful things that you feel he or she can't possible mean? These people have been hurt in such a way that characterizing them as damaged is an under-statement. How do I know this on such a personal level? I knew a few women and young girls who had my same story. They grew up around violence and dysfunction at times. I heard some of these ladies' stories. I once knew this woman who told me about her life and how she had been through so much that she lost everyone she ever loved or tried to love. What happened?

This woman grew up with a mom, aunts, and cousins who lived in the same house. However, somehow she felt invis-ible. She had an unbreakable bond with her cousins, yet they still thought she was crazy because of some of the things she would say and do. Her mom always went out with different men each night and barely had time for her. One of her aunts was a great person but was always consumed with marijuana and alcohol. Another of her aunts was so spiritual that she felt like she could never talk to her because her aunt could not speak to her in layman's terms. The girl's mom would date some jerks, some ballers, and some violent men. Some time these men would stay over, and she would witness them cursing her mom out, blackening her mom's eye, busting her mom's lips, and worst trying and succeeding in raping her mother. The worse situation that occurred was when her mom's boyfriend came over one day. While the mom was in the shower, she was the only one there. The man had his way with her and made her be quiet and told her if she told her mom anything about what had happened, he would kill everybody who stayed in the house. To make it believable, he showed this 9-year-old his gun. This girl grew up into a woman who had so many secrets and so many scars that she never could learn how to allow her scars to heal because so many people came in her life who reminded her of the things that happened. She got pregnant about 7 times throughout her life and aborted all of them because she never wanted a child to go through what she went through. This particular girl felt like the best she could do for a unborn baby is to keep it that way. Coming into a cruel and unjust world would just be wickness. Before she could learn how to heal and recover, she decided to end anything that threaten her to have to forgive and heal. She was in and out of jail for assaulting and battering others because of either how they looked at her or how they talked to her. She had no understanding how many murders she committed by killing someone's spirit by killing their pride, esteem, and confidence and at the time she could care less. She had zero tolerance for anything she felt was offensive. Even when people came in her life who were sincere in loving her, she would push them away because she couldn't trust any of it and was not used to it. This woman to this very day has continued to practice SCREAMING IN SILENCE.

ENCOURAGEMENT

_____

_____

_____

_____

_____

_____

_____

_____

_____

_____

_____

_____

ENCOURAGEMENT

SCREAMING IN SILENCE "THE WANNA BE DADDY'S GIRL"

Now, reading this chapter title should help you know what this story is going to be about, right? A fatherless child who looks for her father's approval or for a relationship with him but rebels when she cannot get it? Well, keep reading! There were two sisters, one of whom lost her dad at the age of 5. He wasn't very active in her life at first, but he came around sometimes. One night while being in a situation he should not have been in, he lost his life to violence and betrayal. The other sister, however, had a present and active father until the age of 7. These two sisters had the same mother but had two different fathers in two different times of their lives. The oldest sister who lost her dad first strove in so many ways to find attention from other male role models. Some ended up being alright, and others ended up being dangerous. She could never get that void filled the way she wanted it to be filled, so one day, she decided to act like he never existed, and she played that part for almost 22 years. At least, she thought she played the part well, and anybody who was watching her from the outside would have thought the same thing except for the fact that the girl was so insecure about every move she made. She doubted everything she did and everything she said. She hated the way she looked, and no one could ever make her feel worthy. These were her inner thoughts she never shared with anybody. Well, that was until she had a little sister who had some of the same feelings.

The sister who also lost her dad at a young age as well was better at hiding her pain and rejection because she hid it behind her voice. What do I mean? Your voice comes off as your confidence along with your movement. Either you talk with confidence or you talk with insecurities. Well, the young girl learned how to talk with such confidence that people would think she had everything she wanted when she wanted it. She was very mannerable, respectful, and well-educated when it came to talking to others. She seemed to have this so-called life figured out. However, this was her well-developed misleading face. Have you ever heard of the saying, "It takes one to know one?" Well, that's what exposed the young girl. See, the older girl knew oh so well of this hurt and pain, and one night the younger sister told the family she was tired and not feeling too well, so she went to her room.

The oldest sister felt like something else was going on so she gave her about 5 minutes to herself, and then she went into her room to check on her. When she went into her room the young girl was passed out. The oldest sister could barely breath in the room. She took her sister to the other room, opened the window, and threw water on her. Suddenly, the sister awoke and said, "What happened?"

She did not know that her older sister was going to explain it from beginning to the end. She was confused. The oldest sister responded, "You know what happened. You inhaled too much of the fumes. Don't try to deny it. See, I've been here and done this. I saw the can of spray paint. You sprayed it in the top and sniffed it until you became numb. I saw mom's gasoline container under your bed with the napkin. You soaked it with the gasoline and put it to your face until you became light headed, and I see the brown paper bag that is also filled with spray paint that you actually inhaled and exhaled. Don't you know you could have killed yourself?" The baby sister cried out and responded, "That was the point!!! I'm tired now. I am tired of acting like I'm alright! The two released their pain with one another about just wanting their fathers to love them enough to be there. The sisters found comfort in each other for that time, and let's just say one of them overcame it, and the other is still SCREAMING IN SILENCE!!!!

REFLECTIONS

_____

_____

_____

_____

_____

_____

_____

_____

_____

_____

_____

REFLECTIONS

SCREAMING IN SILENCE
"THE PINEAPPLE"

Why is it so hard to talk to the ones whom you talk to on a regular basis such as ones you call family and friends? Why is it so very hard to just be completely open with these people about things that have affected you in a way that will no longer allow you to be the same person? Well, sometimes it's not necessarily them. It's you, the one that has been affected with the poison, hurt, and betrayal. How can I say this with such confidence? I know this because of a story I saw closely and personally. I knew a lady who was so gorgeous, but her attitude was one of those attitudes that you could smell miles away. It was the kind of attitude that allowed you only to be able to be around her for seconds if you didn't practice humbleness. When I met this woman, I wanted to know so badly how could someone so beautiful act so ugly, so that's what I did. I made it my business to get to know her, and this is the story of the one I call "Pineapple."

She grew up without a full-time father. Because he wasn't always around, she was one who had to live and learn. She acted hard because of the many things she witnessed from women who always held their guard down. Those are the type of women who practice humbleness, and a lot of people take that for granted. There are other women you see who trust completely in the Lord and allow Him to fight their battles. Well, if you don't look closely, you don't see the effect of trusting God. To someone who is just taking a glimpse, he or she would say God wasn't moving fast enough. That's what happened with this lady. She had a glimpse of so many women go through different things. Her perspective of them was that they were weak, so she made a conscious decision never to be one of them. She worked hard to form these spikes on her surface so whoever got close would get poked before he or she had a chance to poke her. However, she seemed to get involved with men who somehow allowed her to put that border of spikes away.

This woman was capable of putting her spikes away, but it had to be on her time and on her grounds. Unfortunately, the times she put them down allowed her to develop even sharper spikes. From being with men who cheated, treated her as less than a person, hit her, and took part of her identity, she was pushed never to repeat the same behaviors even though she did anyway. What was so interesting about this woman, however, was if you looked hard enough, you saw all her pain. You could see all the scars beneath the makeup, and something made me want to hold her even with the spikes touching me just to show her that I was real and sincere. Every time I saw this woman, I looked at her with remorse, frustration, and understanding. Why did I look at her with understanding?

I understood what it felt like to be hurt so badly that you wanted to hide behind something you are not because you are tired of a feeling that you think will never go away. Most importantly, when I looked at her and I saw hope, because NO ONE WANTS TO FEEL SO MUCH PAIN AND NOT SEE A DOOR OF ESCAPE. MY HOPE FOR HER IS THAT SHE FINDS HER DOOR SO SHE WILL NO LONGER HAVE TO BE SCREAMING IN SILENCE.

PERSONAL PRAYER

_____

_____

_____

_____

_____

_____

_____

_____

_____

_____

_____

_____

_____

PERSONAL PRAYER

_____

_____

_____

_____

_____

_____

_____

_____

_____

_____

_____

_____

SCREAMING IN SILENCE "THE ONE WHO LOST HOPE"

I remember when I was in high school, and I talked to this girl who was in the 10th grade like me. She was more popular than I was, but somehow she made me feel like she looked up to me. We talked almost everyday in school and then again at night. Eventually we got really close. I remember this one Saturday morning I was talking to her, and she sounded so sad. I asked her what was wrong, and she told me she was just tired of holding so much in. I asked her what did she mean, and she told me nevermind. I gave her a little of the history I saw and experienced, and with that one solid and raw moment, she became like a overflowing tear bank. She was crying uncontrollably, and when I could finally help calm her down, she shared only part of her story about how she got to a point in her life in which she just lost hope. This girl was so beautiful. She was my ideal size, and her smile gave you a sense that good people were still out there in spite of the things you might have been through. Well, that was only on the outside because on the inside, she was SCREAMING IN SILENCE."

She came from a household that had a mom, dad, and siblings. From the outside, her parents were awesome, and she and her siblings were so close that you would not have thought anything abnormal went on in this house. Some of the events that happened to her in this house from a very small age until her high school days would amaze you. She was the youngest of her household, and she was also the quietest. In this house, she was being sexually abused by one of her siblings. She told me how it all started one day when she was playing house, a game that a lot of young children played. She saw a side of one of her siblings she didn't want to see. She went on to tell me how her sister started kissing on her, and rubbing on her vagina. It didn't feel right to her, but her sister told her it was because she loved her. Years went on, and she was in 4th grade, and the activities between her sister and her didn't stop at that time. She shared with me how her sister would call her in the room when all the other siblings were away to come suck on her breast or rub her vagina. I remember her telling me when her sister would call her, it was in a demeanor like she was asking her to come scratch her back or help her clean the room. She never shared any of this with her other siblings, and when she got in 5th grade, it finally stopped not because her sister knew it was wrong but because her sister became more sexually active with different boys.

The story didn't stop there, however. Even with that going on most of her elementary school life, she then got involved with a crowd in middle school that smoked marijuana and did other stuff that would allow them to avoid reality of what was going on in their lives. Although these party moments helped her not feel anything at the moment, she felt worse than what she felt before and after the high was over. I wondered how were these girls getting marijuana and alcohol as middle school students. It was a process. What do I mean? I'll tell you. One of the other girls with whom she was smoking with had a hook up, but the hook up required work. They would have to go over this guy's house and do whatever he asked of them if they wanted the marijuana badly enough. The question was, "How far was she willing to go?" Well, because of what transpired between her sister and her like having to suck on her sister breasts all the time or giving her oral sex, she felt like it couldn't be any worse doing it to guys. At least the guys didn't put on an act and pretend to be one way while being another. If they wanted sex, they said they wanted sex. If they wanted oral sex, they said they wanted oral sex. If they wanted threesomes, they said they wanted threesomes. For the most part, she and her new crew did most of these things, and no one ever knew. She lost hope in guys, too, because so many of these guys who looked so innocent and looked like they would never hurt a fly were somehow taking advantage of these young girls.

Eventually, the girl pulled away from this group. She lost her mom before she went in high school, and after praying that God wouldn't take her mom and would heal her, she ended up dying which caused her to lose hope in God, too. Well, coming back to the day she told me all these things, there were a few things she told me that would blow ones mind, but vowing not to ever tell anyone, I just told her I would always be there for her. A few years went past, and I remember her calling me with the same hurt and pain in her voice. She told me how she had a house party one night, and some friends came over and ate and played a few games. The people were all familiar faces and were people she had known for years. One minute she remembered dancing, and the next minute she just remember waking up sore in her bed with blood all over her sheets and nothing else. She hated to believe that of all her friends who were there did not prevent her from being drugged and raped because that's what everything pointed to. She called a few of them crying and trying to figure things out what happened, but no one said a word. She went to the emergency room, and the doctor confirmed to her everything she thought actually had happened. From that day forward, she told me she absolutely had nothing else to lose. These were supposed to be her close friends with whom she grew up. She never said a word to anyone about what the doctors said or the fact that no one ever came clean with her. Throughout the years, she felt as though she lost so much of herself, but losing hope was something completely different. Today, if you see her, she smiles and laughs, but you would never know the emptiness she feels inside. After all, she is SCREAMING, YET SHE IS SCREAMING IN SILENCE!!!

ENCOURAGEMENT

ENCOURAGEMENT

_____

_____

_____

_____

_____

_____

_____

_____

_____

_____

_____

_____

SCREAMING IN SILENCE "THE ONE WHO DIDN'T MAKE IT"

I didn't know this girl, but I new her story oh so well. Have you ever been in a situation in which you felt like you were being done wrong or felt like you didn't "think" you should have been treated that way? You had no one else to talk to because they wouldn't understand where you are coming from, so you had to paint a picture, a beautiful picture for someone. I know sometimes in life when your life is so upside down and you are hurting tremendously to the point that you couldn't imagine someone else understanding that hurt, you may feel the need to get the paint brush or the makeup out and just begin to paint a beautiful masterpiece. This masterpiece is filled with laughter, jokes, remarkable smiles, and a giving heart. This is what you create when you are hiding or screaming in silence. Well, this girl I heard of had been doing it for so long. Then, she met a man, and the man seemed like he could fix her. He seemed like he could take the broken pieces of her and kiss them and mend her back together. The two became very close, and they felt in love. At least, she thought it was love. After all, she never ever really was taught what love was. She assumed she was in love compared things to movies and what she saw from other people, but she never really knew what it actually felt like.

She thought she had finally found true love until one day she received a busted lip from this man. She went three whole days walking past her mirror in her house asking herself, "Is this what love feels like?" Everytime she asked herself that question, the man would appear suddenly and apologize. He cried and told her he didn't mean it. He swore that he would never hurt her because he never loved anyone as much as he loved her. Every day and night for those three days, the girl battled within and asked herself, "Is this right?" However, her answer would remain the same, "I know he loves me because I can see it in his tears." Well, this cycle continued for 1 ½ years. The girl suffered from head injuries, back injuries, broken jaws, and broken wrists; however, she never left because his story never changed.

She would try to talk to different people who she thought were her friends. At first, it seemed to make her feel better until they began to tell her to leave. Sometimes, she would get the strength to pack her children and herself up. Then, hesitation would creep in just long enough for him to catch her trying to leave. In the process of her being caught, he would beat her like she was a man and then explain to her how the friends with whom she spoke are not really her friends because if they were, they would tell her to stick with her man. Eventually, the girl just shut down. She didn't talk to anybody about anything, and if her friends asked her anything, her response would be, "I have a plan, and I'm leaving soon." Sadly, she never applied that plan to her life.

One evening, her close friend had been calling her all day and wasn't getting an answer, so she decided to surprise the girl and bring her lunch. When she arrived at her home, she saw that the door was cracked, so she went in and called her name, She didn't get an answer so she went to the girl's room and found her. She was beaten to death in front of her mirror in her room. She wasn't breathing, and from the looks of her body, she had been that way for a few days. All her friend saw was broken pieces of her mirror with blood on them, and the glass all over her head. When the paramedics arrived, they told her friend that she had been gone for almost 63 hours. The girl had been dead for about three days. I didn't know the girl, but I knew her story oh so well. She was a victim and did not know it. She thought she knew what love was, but she never was taught what it looks like. She wanted to see the best in everybody, but she did not know that everyone is not good for her, and she did not know how to run for help. Like I said, I know the story oh so well. So many women hide this story. THEY SCREAM, AND SCREAM, AND SCREAM FOR HELP. THE ONLY PROBLEM IS THEY ARE "SCREAMING IN SILENCE.

REFLECTIONS

REFLECTIONS

BRIGHTER DAYS IN THE SCREAMING

Every story that I have told you has been of young ladies who have been screaming in silence for so many different reasons. Believe it or not, that's not even half of their stories, but I don't want you to think that their stories all ended that way. I know we always want to believe in the happily ever after and sometimes that isn't the case. "Many are called but few are chosen" was what I was always brought on, and maybe you too. I challenge you to look a little deeper at those words. See, there was a woman I knew, and this woman was called. She was called over and over again, and she was also chosen, but she didn't know that. She didn't know how much of a calling she had over her life. All she really knew was failure, disappointment, deceit, perpetration and dysfunction. However, she had experienced something like no other. She experienced the feeling of the Holy Spirit. She felt it after giving her life back to Christ, and the way she explained this feeling was more than any type of high, love, or human emotion she had ever felt. The feeling she had she told people was worth all the hell she had ever experienced. As she got deeper with God, she realized that her worship was one of her gifts. What she told people was because she was a new creature, she could appreciate everything she went through because to feel that much hurt and all of a sudden feel a powerful move of God allowed her to appreciate everything she ever had experienced. This woman learned how to break the chain of SCREAMING IN SILENCE and so can you! Ask me how I know!!!.

PERSONAL PRAYER

PERSONAL PRAYER

_____

_____

_____

_____

_____

_____

_____

_____

_____

_____

_____

_____

_____

WELL...UNTIL NEXT TIME...

TO HEAR HER STORY FULLY , JUST REFLECT ON EVERY-
THING YOU HAVE RECEIVED OUT OF THIS BOOK. I KNOW
THAT SOMETIMES THE PAIN HURTS SO MUCH THAT WE
DON'T FEEL LIKE PUSHING. WE DON'T FEEL LIKE MOVING
FORWARD. WE MAY FEEL LIKE WE HAVE BEEN CURSED,
BUT LOOK AT THESE WOMEN. THEY ALL BEEN THROUGH
SOMETHING AND ALTHOUGH SOME OF THEM LEARNED
TO STOP SCREAMING IN SILENCE, SOME ARE STILL TRY-
ING TO GET THERE. THE POINT IS YOU CAN MAKE IT. NO
MATTER HOW BAD IT SEEMS AND NO MATTER HOW HOR-
RIFYING IT IS TO FACE, YOU CAN PUT YOUR ACTING DAYS
UP. YOU DON'T HAVE TO PAINT A PICTURE YOU THINK EV-
ERYBODY WANTS TO SEE, BUT YOU CAN SHOW THEM THE
REAL YOU. EVENTUALLY WITH OVERCOMING, THE BEAU-
TY IS THAT SMILE YOU WORKED SO HARD TO PUSH OUT
TO HIDE THE PAIN. IT BECOMES REAL, AND IT BECOMES
SINCERE. IT BECOMES A TESTAMENT OF YOU OVERCOM-
ING WHATEVER CAME YOUR WAY. THAT IS THE MOMENT
WHEN YOU REALIZE THAT TRULY WHAT DOESN'T KILL
YOU REALLY DOES MAKE YOU STRONGER, WISER, MORE
POWERFUL, HAPPIER, AND A OVERCOMER. TO ALL OF MY
S.I.S., BY THE TIME YOU FINISH READING THIS, MY HOPE
FOR YOU IS THAT WE ARE NO LONGER CONSIDER S.I.S.
"SCREAMING IN SILENCE," BUT INSTEAD, WE ARE COM-
ING TOGETHER ALL OVER THE WORLD "SCREAMING IN

POWER." DUST THE TRIALS, PAIN, AND NAYSAYERS OFF AND GET UP AND OWN YOUR HAPPINESS. DON'T COMPARE YOURSELF TO WHAT YOU THINK SOMEBODY ELSE HAS AND HOW THEY MAY BE SO MUCH BETTER OFF THAN YOU. INSTEAD, COMPOSE YOURSELF TO YOURSELF. LOOK AT YOUR LIFE. I MEAN REALLY LOOK AT EVERY BROKEN PIECE AND EVERY SECRET PIECE AND FACE IT HEAD ON. COMPOSE WHAT IT IS YOU WANT FROM IT FROM EVERY JOURNEY YOU HAVE BEEN ON. MAKE A CONSCIOUS DECISION THAT YOU ARE GOING TO LET EVERYTHING THAT HAS EVER HAPPENED TO YOU MAKE A BETTER YOU AND YOU GET UP AND SPREAD SOME GOOD NEWS TO OTHERS WHO NEED TO HEAR YOUR STORY. OTHERS NEED TO KNOW IT'S A RAINBOW COMING. OTHERS JUST NEED TO KNOW THEY DIDN'T GO THROUGH CIRCUMSTANCES BY THEMSELVES. DO YOU REALLY KNOW WHO YOU ARE? YOU ARE MADE TO WIN, DEFEAT OBSTACLES, AND RISE ABOVE ANYTHING. IF I CAN DO IT, BELIEVE ME, I KNOW THAT YOU CAN. I ASKED YOU IN THE VERY BEGINNING A QUESTION, AND IF YOU ARE LIKE ME THE ANSWER WITH ALL HOPE HAS CHANGED.

DEAR S.I.S

HOW ARE YOU DOING? HOW ARE YOU REALLY DOING? FINALLY SIS LET ME ASK YOU THIS DIRECT QUESTION

DEAR S.I.S.

SCREAMING IN SILENCE?

ENCOURAGEMENT

_____

_____

_____

_____

_____

_____

_____

_____

_____

_____

_____

ENCOURAGEMENT

REFLECTIONS